. . . And Softly Teach

...And Softly Teach

Francis Lewis

A. & C. Black Limited · London

First published in this edition 1971 by A. & C. Black Ltd.

ISBN 0 7136 1195 2

Printed in Great Britain by
The Whitefriars Press Ltd., London & Tonbridge

Editorial

Achievements in Teaching has been designed as a series
of reports written by teachers describing their teaching
in such a personal style and in such fine detail as to enable
other members of the profession to appreciate the interplay
between teaching techniques and educational values.

The reports, therefore, differ greatly from those in
which personal differences between teachers are averaged
out in attempts to measure the effectiveness of a particular
method or set of materials. In *Achievements in Teaching*
the personality of the teacher counts: the style of the man
is shown by the way in which he works in the classroom,
emphasising this or that value, choosing this or that
method of approach, with a preference for certain kinds
of material and the use of his own carefully thought out
criteria for evaluating the evidence provided by his pupils
within the intimacy of the special relationship built up
between teacher and pupils in the classroom.

Yet these expressions of personality are cloaked by
pseudonyms. There are good reasons for this. No teacher
is an island. If he is to talk freely about his own work
he must be able to do so without involving publicly
others who may in varying degrees have supported or
opposed his venture. Moreover, since these reports are
concerned with work on the frontier of educational
advance, in the sense that what has been attempted has
been unorthodox at least in the place where it was
attempted, it is important that untypical practices should
not be publicly identified with particular localities.

The reports published in this series have a special
relevance for the contemporary educational scene since
they focus closely on the teacher at work with his class.
Thus they present a kind of writing that is essential to all

who are seriously concerned, as are so many today, with problems of curriculum renewal and with the improvement of human relations in school. Teachers and researchers alike can profitably use reports that sharpen awareness of what may be involved in attempts to implement educational values in the complex situations provided by live teachers working with live children in actual classrooms. In selecting reports for inclusion in this series care has been taken to choose those which can be seen to have this general contemporary relevance irrespective of their particular local setting and time.

The editorial board gratefully acknowledges its debt to those who have, in spite of the ruling about anonymity, agreed to contribute to this series. Thanks are also offered to the Research Committee of the Institute and Faculty of Education of the University of Newcastle upon Tyne which has sponsored this venture in the hope that it will make a useful contribution to the advancement of the study of education.

. . . And Softly Teach

Townend Estate is a pre-war housing estate on the edge of the town. It was opened with the present school in the years between the wars to house people moved from a slum clearance area. Most of the children come from this older housing, some from newer houses nearby. Inevitably the socially more successful families move to better and newer estates and so Townend is well known as a poor area. Nevertheless few of the homes are needy and the children look quite well kept and are reasonably clean. Some parents are unemployed, either through lack of jobs or chronic unwillingness to work, though the numbers are not really large.

The school's task of looking after its 490 children is not easy. As can be imagined, many children have difficult parents, more conscious of their rights than their duties. For serious misdemeanours in school corporal punishment may be used. Parents and children resent this and angry visits by mothers are not unknown.

Academic standards are not high in the school—last year only two children went on to grammar schools, though more will find themselves in GCE streams of secondary modern schools. The school is not well equipped with books. There is no central school library. Each class is loaned three or four dozen books, mainly from the public library, which are usually more suitable for able children. Since there was no fourth year C stream last year, the present 4C is unusually badly equipped. This is my class. Our 'library books' are on loan from a second year class; our supplementary readers were donated by other teachers from their surplus stock and, while not all are tattered, most are unsuitable. Recently a few dozen supplementary readers and library books have been chosen for us and ordered, although the head, perhaps understandably, is extremely reluctant to give us anything new or valuable since the children are very destructive.

The classroom we now occupy is large with a good deal of locker and storage space, and has a useful store-room attached. This accommodation—part of a three-room pre-fab block—is an undoubted advantage. Unfortunately it is sited well away from the supervised playground and the main school. The rather long route along which the children pass to and from the school gives many opportunities for mischief. At playtimes and lunchtimes it has been impossible, so far, to keep all the children away from the unsupervised huts and a good deal of mischief, pilfering and even vandalism has occurred during those times. The head has decided that, unless these out-of-lesson-time misbehaviours stop forthwith, we are to move into the main school. This would be a great setback since in every way but situation the school rooms are inferior to the huts.

The home background of many of the children makes for unsettled and sometimes unstable personalities. Several come from broken homes, but more come from homes with too many children for weak parents to manage or with feckless parents who, say the children, 'are never in'. One child casually tells of his daily lunch, 'a boiled egg at Gran's', another of fights at home and of being told not to come back. In having difficulties such as these the children are not much worse off than many others who fit easily into a school and co-operate with their teachers. For many children such threats, blows and insecurity are commonplace. But to account for their poor social attitudes and the immaturity of children in 4C it is necessary to see their record as a class.

Here, I think, we must face the possibility that the system may have failed them badly. What happened to this class before they came to me is not known directly. There is also the added complication that the present head has been newly appointed. However, as the past experience of my class is part of my present problem, I have tried to piece the story together from fragments of talks with teachers. Doubtless in many details the picture is inadequate but in its main outline I have good reason to believe that it is substantially true.

In their first year in the junior school the children are said to have 'had a student' much of the time. This is not uncommon because of the Local Education Authority's extreme staffing difficulties, and more often than not 'having a student' means that the class was looked after by a young boy or girl waiting to go to college. To put such hard-to-manage children as these were when very young, according to the infant headteachers, in the hands of an untrained person would seem to me to have no real justification.

In their second year their teacher was a qualified, competent woman, kind and friendly, but unfortunately she was seriously ill during the year and away from school for several months. While she was away the children were shared out amongst other classes until there was someone free to take them.

In their third year their teacher was an untrained graduate; this was his first class and, in his determination to maintain strict discipline in a class now acknowledged in the school to be a problem class, he used the cane as the recognised instrument of corporal punishment. Again, continuity of contact between teacher and class was frequently broken since it was standard practice in this school for the teacher of what was then 3C to be called on to take any other class whose teacher was absent and for his children to be shared out among other classes. Since the staff seems to have had a good deal of absence at this time, the class must have had a very disturbed history.

This, then, is the background story of staffing difficulties and the resultant policies that may have contributed much to the unmanageability and poor attitudes of the class, of children not in themselves bad.

When this year they became 4C the twenty-four children who form the bulk of the class were supplemented by six outsiders from the B stream. This little group contains some of the most difficult and disturbing members of the class.

The original group lacks self-discipline and responsibility but they are, with exceptions, easily likable as individuals and could, in time, settle into a rough but co-operative group. The new boys, on the other hand, are more like real problem children. Their homes are poor and several have police records. Their initial hostility towards myself was much more deliberate and ingeniously expressed. They are, in fact, more intelligent than most of the others who simply ignore adults, while these openly reject them.

One of the contributing reasons for their disturbed state is not hard to see. The head agrees that this class contains not only children with low intelligence scores but also children who have been put there because of poor behaviour. There is, he says, 'not much in it between 4C and 4B, but yours are the bad ones . . .' This seems especially true of the six ex-Bs, and they are clever enough to resent it. Had they gone—as they might have, had they not consistently under-achieved—to 4B, they would very likely have been easier now to live with. They very much resent being put down into 4C which everyone knows has such inferior children. This group then is a seriously disturbing element in an already difficult group.

To me it seems strange that it was not realised that mixing these children in a notoriously difficult class was a serious mistake and one that need never have been made since 4B has only thirty mild quiet children in it with an understanding teacher. However, what I see as a mistake is certainly not recognised as such by the head who claims that the present 4C is not more disturbed or difficult than the old 3C, while the present 4B has been freed from the encumbrance of laggards and potential troublemakers.

The poverty of experience of the children's three years in the junior department can be illustrated in another way.

Almost any reference made by them to their teachers, other than rudely, has been to those in their infant years. So often the children have said 'We did it in Miss L's class,' or 'We went there with Miss L,' that I can almost believe that growth, certainly happiness, ended when they left the infant school.

From the first day of term I kept a diary in which I recorded material bearing on the attitudes of these children both to discipline and to learning, and I have drawn on this diary to fix as far as possible some of the main points in the very gradual, but nevertheless quite undeniable, progress made during the year. Here, to begin with, are a few extracts from early days. (All the children, of course, have been given pseudonyms to make it impossible for the school or individual children to be identified.)

September 9

Is forming a line in the yard in a crowd of 450 others an impossible task for these children? The effort to achieve it and then walk the length of the path to the classroom, as the school assembles at the beginning of the morning or afternoon or after play, seems to produce a stressful situation that results in displays of bad temper. Today the girls started picking on Albert and there was some fighting and crying. Peter Cole got to the room two minutes before me with several other boys (I was settling another quarrel) and had beaten them up by the time I arrived. Jimmy McDougall was howling. Peter Cole said they called him names; I believe him, but he provokes them. So we had not even begun the day and good humour had gone.

September 21

Some were willing to clear up a little after painting,

though several (Robertson, Gray and Green) refused point blank. They would rather not paint (or do craft, or draw, or anything else), so it is no good saying 'No clearing up, no painting!' I seemed to get some progress in the room and went out to see what was happening at the sinks in the toilet; several children had come back wet, one crying. The toilets were awash, several jars broken, lights on, etc. I had told only two or three to do the job, but others slip out while I am occupied.

September 24

Today the caretaker complained he had to remove several milk bottles from the lavatory pans. My boys obviously. He also mentioned other incidents he hadn't wanted to bother me with—he's very tolerant and helpful. It appears they climb on the roof at night, have several times painted swear words, etc., in the toilets, and he sees them smoking behind the huts (?David Gray).

October 15

For three weeks we have been saving up to buy a hamster. The loss of the rabbit through its broken leg was really felt. Today I brought the hamster to school and the headteacher reluctantly gave us the school's cage. At lunchtime a crowd of hysterically excited boys came to the staffroom to say that the hamster was dead—was bleeding etc., etc. I got to the room, sending everyone away, and found the hamster had in fact been stabbed through with scissors. I drowned it. This was a dreadful day. I collected all the boys who had been in the hut (to go in is forbidden, but eight had been—I am refused a door key!). It seemed certain that Peter Cole did it, although he denied it violently, being alternately nasty, then sullen and

muttering. He admitted going in but said he 'looked
at the rat but only gave it food . . .' The head heard
about it and took action, caning several boys for
being in the huts. He intends moving us into the main
school and says that though I have tried this is the
end . . .

October 19

The violence seems worse than ever. George Baxter
kicked Joseph Banks in the stomach when they were
in the hall with the head yesterday. Banks could not
reach home walking, he 'collapsed at the end of the
street' according to his mother and is now in a
wheelchair—she muttered about rupture, being
crippled, etc. She thinks I ignored his crying but
today was the first I heard of it. I just don't get time
to follow up each crying child. George Baxter was
with the head for half an hour, he came over to the
classroom seeming frozen—whitefaced and staring.
Eventually I got over to talk to him and he insisted
over and over 'Will they put me away? They'll put
me on probation,' etc. He is actually one of the less
cruel boys, but uncontrollably stupid.

November 3

More thieving. These last few days things disappearing
include sweets from my drawer, every single bead and
brooch we had collected as costume, money, odds
and ends from desks, and I saw Peter Cole disappearing
with bulging pockets—a sheet of coloured silk I had
borrowed for the play. Yesterday I loaned out two
new vices which I had just bought for woodwork.
Five minutes later Harold Smith had hammered and
bent one of them until it was useless. To prevent this
destruction there should be one boy to one teacher.
While I am settling a crisis, or a frenzied child, in one

part of the room, others break out elsewhere. We get nowhere.

To make a start with a problem class in a school one knows well is difficult enough; to take such a class in a new school increases the hazards considerably. Moreover, although as a newcomer I could quite reasonably have expected to have been informed of the class beforehand, to have seen records and to have heard serious discussion and constructive comment, this did not happen. The staff paid me the doubtful compliment of expecting me to hold the class down for a year or else put up with them, but any requests for help in the form of information or constructive suggestion have produced for the most part only generalised comments expressing dissatisfaction and condemnation of these unfortunate children.

Why should this be so? I can recall several instances in the staffroom where the conversation has momentarily touched off a serious discussion of problem children in schools in difficult areas. These discussions have always gone the same way. Colleagues have unanimously agreed that, although a bad home can cause a problem child, the school is not the place in which to try to compensate for some of the home's inadequacies. And yet, of course, most of the same teachers are making this allegedly futile attempt willingly and cheerfully every day. Perhaps it is only when the children's behaviour reaches a critically low standard that sympathy and understanding are abandoned and we find ourselves avoiding the problem, rejecting and condemning the children, or even lashing out blindly in our attempts to control a situation that seems to be so hopelessly out of control.

Doubtless I was aware of this before September of this year, but I cannot recall a school situation in which such knowledge was so relevant. My return to teaching after a year's absence in study was not a help. A rusty teacher at a

8

new school is not the quickest person to respond to a demanding situation. It takes time to realise the depth of a problem, still longer to find any solution to it. Children's fundamental needs may always be pretty much the same but our ways of satisfying them will be very different.

The first three weeks of September in my new classroom seemed an endless chaos. I was unable to discern who were the truly violent children and to distinguish them from those who, involved in violence, were merely fighting, literally fighting, for survival. Every playtime and lunch-time, and at any time when I did not keep the children strictly pinned down in their seats, there would be a brawl with boys holding boys by the throat and girls crying. There could be no reliance on the listlessness, apathy or fatigue of older or less intelligent children. To me they seemed to be in a frenzy of meaningless destruction. It was a situation that I could see I was precipitating and, while it was certainly bad, I am convinced it was necessary. The violence of those first weeks had to be tolerated or crushed; there was very little one could do to channel or contain it.

It was obvious to the children from the start that a new regime had arrived with myself. In the first few minutes of the first day they demanded to know if I was going to cane them. It was not a meaningless question for the sake of talking. There followed a torrent, a flood of stories of being caned, of angry mothers, of crudeness and resentment. For several weeks following they tried to find out if I meant those earlier words about caning. Many times since, when my exasperation has shown, someone has called out 'Well, why don't you cane us?' My obvious good intentions and desire to be kind were the children's chief hold over me and, as was to be expected, they made good use of it.

To be firm without being violent is not easy in the face of thirty lively ten-year-olds skilled in non-co-operation and resentful of the authority they badly need. These necessary virtues are then a handicap and a compromise

9

has continually to be found. I was conscious of little of this in my first fortnight. From my diary it stands out clearly that in those early days the chaos and turmoil seemed to me total and meaningless. Then, during the fourth week, I began to see who the trouble-makers were. It became apparent that some eight or nine boys were the real storm centre and that the rest were merely taking advantage of the storm or struggling to survive it.

In such a situation, as problem-laden for them as for me, it is obvious that the children were not ready for deliberate learning either from activities or through listening. It was not to be expected that in a room where for the first time the cane would not be used, they would freely, even in a small degree, co-operate in learning.

Our earliest activities were centred on animals. A child brought her neglected rabbit to school to give to the class. She daily threatened to take it home when anyone else held or fed it, but by the end of a week it had become class property and of real interest to most of them. We talked a good deal about it and rabbits in general; they collected food for it and cleaned its quarters out more often than was necessary. This willingness to play an active rôle in looking after animals has been an outstanding charac-teristic of the children. It has applied to most tasks offered them, even where animals were not concerned. But, as yet, there has been no carry-over into written work or records and I have thought it wrong to make a burden of what will in time come naturally, with encouragement.

In the second week after the arrival of the rabbit a girl took fright while holding it and threw it violently at the floor. The rabbit's leg was broken and a week later it died. For a short time the rabbit had been a valuable asset to the class and it had not died through being unloved. Many of these children find it difficult to live with anything weaker than themselves. Their clumsiness can often look like cruelty but it arises, as is the case with very young children, from an inability to see the animal's point of view and needs, rather than from a desire to hurt.

October 15

At lunchtime today something of a lessening perhaps in rowdiness and bickering in the group which I had taken with me on a quick trip to a nearby park. None of the group is really better than the next—there is always someone to create havoc. Gordon Bell today had to be sent back—he would not let anyone fish and then began chasing through the roses. I had to send him off, although this made him impossible to handle for the rest of the day. It is strange that they should be such poor fishermen—they *say* they do catch fish but have no real idea of watching quietly while they make the attempt. David Gray and Gerald Brown are probably best and they are among the most mature, though toughest. The rest just splash about and shriek when they see anything.

Another of our daily activities has centred round this pool in the park. In the earlier days I allowed a few hangers-on to come in with me to inspect the pool in the lunch hour. It immediately became the highlight of the day and we have visited it each day since. If I expected that in order to do something they desperately wanted to do the children would for a short time behave, even organise themselves sufficiently to pursue a simple pleasing activity, I was wrong. Every day each group—for I soon split them into groups of apparent friends—wrangled, fought, shouted abuse and spoiled one another's fishing without any breaks.

This pond visit is still, after seven weeks, their favourite pursuit and, although I cannot claim that they have settled in to any study or even much interest in the life of the pond, they are considerably less violent whilst there, and their knowledge, casually picked up, is much greater.

We very quickly began an aquarium from our catches.

Each lunch-hour it is re-stocked and over-stocked for, like infants, they will not believe that there is a limit to the number of fish we can keep. There is again no desire to hurt the creatures, but frequently I find fish splashed on to the floor by children unable to keep their hands out of the water. Less frequently now do we have milk, or painting water, poured into the tank. It has not been possible, so far, to get the simplest study of the processes of pond life going, nor are they willing to help find names from reference books I provide, still less to read facts about them.

Viewing their behaviour and attitudes as a whole I do not find this surprising or disappointing. I am constantly being made aware that in matters such as this they are infantile. For them the immediate present is everything. They must 'do it now' for it to have meaning. For instance, there is a daily fight to get at my net for fishing. I have suggested they buy sixpenny ones—they do not lack the money—or else that they should make them, and two have done so quite simply, but the others prefer, it seems, the daily squabble for a five-minute ration of my net.

However, with the passage of time there are definite signs of possible improvement in their attitudes. Daily I notice details of behaviour that point to a happier future, but, as yet, the general outline of activity is very poor. They will listen to me, for short periods, talking about our animals (we keep frogs, a toad, spiders and worms as well), but to find anything out for themselves, or to note down anything observed, other than to copy down from the blackboard, is still beyond them.   ·

There is, of course, the veiled-threat way of compelling what is curiously termed 'observation'—'Make a sentence up about today's catch and we will go into the park again tomorrow,'—but, as I have frequently remarked, the attitudes of these children are such that they reject what they badly want if it entails effort and there is an easy alternative. When on occasions I have tentatively tried such an approach in other matters they have in effect said 'No'. Obviously I can, for short periods, compel an activity centred on these things, but I believe little is lost in proceeding more slowly and that ultimately this approach will be more fruitful.

October 22

When I first came here a colleague told me, 'You can't put anything up on the walls with that class. They immediately tear it down.' They *do* tear it down still, but not immediately; in time they may value their own work; ultimately others' too. It is true, as I am always being told, that they destroy or damage whatever they come into contact with. I hear that Peter Cole and David Gray were knocking down walls when they disappeared from the group on an outing last Saturday. It is an exaggeration, I'm sure, and the walls were derelict broken-down drystone walls any-way but the attitude is typical. The waste of materials in the classroom is only limited by their non-availability, but out of the waste we do increasingly get worthwhile things. Certainly I could not accept as an alternative a cell-like classroom—a peaceful, waste-free desert.

It would perhaps be as well to examine at this point the reasons why we do follow activities such as this. They appear to produce nothing, and I am frequently asked by other members of the staff, 'Why do you do it when they are so awful?' We have, it seems to me, to be constantly setting against the present undesirable behaviour with its destructiveness, even with its cruelty, the possibilities for the future immanent in our approach. Many animals have died, directly and indirectly, as a result of coming into our care. But there is something more than just the present misery and loss. A similar argument applies to property

13

and materials, although it is easier to decide that so many trees, fences or books shall be abused than that as many animals should be made uncomfortable, even killed.

The pond visits are a good example of this. Why do something so little productive of 'good'? We do not go for information or for a starting point for classroom activities as might normally be the case, although both these aspects are minimally present. We do not even go to provide an occasion for getting on with each other. This too would be a possible reason since so many of the factors that create friction and violence are removed—large numbers, obvious enemies, boredom, too much freedom or too many petty restrictions. But the children see to it that I do not at these times try for too much good behaviour too quickly. Although they enjoy being there so much, they will not permit me to use this as a bargaining point for reasonable, to me acceptable, behaviour. When, for example, a child has behaved intolerably he is sent away. I have tried to think of an example of intolerable behaviour but it is, of course, impossible since the point at which the child is removed is the end of a long string of offences—throwing away a catch made by another *and* running through the rose bushes *and* splashing other children deliberately.

If I tend to insist on the unreasonableness of these acts too soon the old hostility arises that was so noticeable in the class in September. Much more than is reasonable has to be tolerated. When I have been forced into saying to a child 'That's enough. Go!', there has been a worsening of my relationship with the group as a whole—even with those I had hoped I was protecting. It is as though the others are aware of being nearly as bad as the one expelled and are aggrieved by his fate. In short, they refuse to be bargained with—I either put up with all, or nothing. In the things they do they might often look as though they are having me on or trying to see how far they can go. Perhaps they do, but I do not believe it always is so. They genuinely do not see a limit to bad behaviour.

14

As I write I realise how much this situation has improved; it has helped in thinking myself back into these sessions to find out now how much more hold over them I now have, how much more amenable they are. For this, I think, is the reason why I have put up with so much from them—doing things with them is much the same as putting up with them. It is not a very high-sounding motive. But to be able to get a place in the children's scheme of things in order that in the future I might be able to guide and influence them more positively is enough and any other benefits are fringe ones. I do now have a greater hold over them. If they do not yet see the value of co-operation with each other, and myself, they are much more willing that gross misbehaviour should be stopped.

This then has been the aim and the end of our first half-term: to put them in a situation, not where they could learn, but where they could become willing to be influenced. We have, I think, been sufficiently successful for more guidance to be possible at least some of the time.

October 26

Last night we went to the beach—a mixed group of six; none of the seriously difficult ones was there. All enjoyed it, though I had to spend most of my time disciplining them to ensure their survival. The beach is a fine place for interest, but not the safest, I should think. It is hard to say what they got out of it; they are certainly no warmer towards me away from school—I felt rather like the driver than a member of the party. We walked the beach collecting shells, pebbles, odd objects of all kinds (I did the collecting —they were not interested), climbed the cliffs, watched ships and so on. George Baxter came down the cliff to a sheer drop. Luckily he stopped for me when I shouted, but he saw no danger even after I pointed the drop out to him. On Thursday another group is going to the moors; perhaps that will be more suitable.

In the first weeks with 4C I realised that I was getting little actual contact with the children as individuals or in small groups. I was so completely occupied by class discipline, in settling and preventing quarrels, that I got no time for talking or for teaching individuals. To this end I arranged a series of out-of-school trips by car to local places of interest. These places would allow for interests to be followed if they arose, but would also permit contact as a group. I chose a moorland expanse, a local peak and a seaside cliff and rock-pool area. The places were not chosen primarily for study or to produce recorded work, although both of these things were suggested and urged on the children before and after the visits. Local works might have been more obvious sites for such activities, but they would not have produced nearly so much play and talk.

Only one group took up the suggestion of simple records. This group happened to comprise the six ex-B-stream children mentioned earlier. This was by far the most difficult group—unwilling to be controlled, to listen or to be directed—but it did help in labelling finds, painting pictures about the trip, even writing a short account of it. The other three groups would do none of this. I had to collect any of the bits of evidence of where we had been which we brought back. They told a few anecdotes about the trip to the class, but were hardly interested enough in the pebbles or sheep-bones collected to display them. And yet, of course, they nag constantly to go again.

November 6

Craft this morning went very well indeed. The oddments of wood and nails were just what the boys need. Some peculiar things were turned out— several blocks nailed together, no sawing, and labelled 'A tank'. In time they will master the material more, I suppose; clay is our most successful medium yet. The ten girls do seem neglected in craft; but then the whole class is boy-orientated, I am afraid. None, boy or girl, is willing (yet?) to do the normal things one expects in craft lessons—models, cardboard, painting puppets, etc. Activities have to be big and unrefined. It certainly makes the classroom exciting first thing in a morning though.

On coming into the classroom first thing in a morning the children would from the start go to the aquarium, cages and other objects of interest round the room. Some merely played, of course, but it seemed a pity to waste the interest of twenty or more because ten did not care. Gradually, however, even those who were not interested at this time began later to draw, to colour, and eventually to attempt some simple craft. From this spontaneous activity has grown the tradition of giving the first session over to work, roughly labelled craft. I set out a permanent painting area and arranged a few desks for clay and other more passing interests.

Most mornings many of the children will get on with such activities, though the response varies. Sometimes they arrive in a more than usual state of irritability, which will have made itself obvious in the assembly, and the first period is merely chaos. If there is nothing they choose to do, then they refuse to be directed. I decide daily whether there is sufficient voluntary activity going on to be worth continuing or whether too many boys are refusing to be caught by anything.

It is difficult to argue the good in this state of affairs to unbelievers, but the standard of discipline, of activity and of consideration shown to others has improved enough

17

ustify it to myself. It would be wrong to think that this
ss could have been ordered to concentrate on any one
ing, such as sums, to start the morning.

November 13

Gordon Bell quite unreasonable. I tried to discuss his
recent behaviour again with him at playtime, to
point out how it hampers us in everything we try to
do. He was rather sullen, though not offensively so.
After play he came back much more cheerful, quite
friendly. He resents correction bitterly, but perhaps
this sort of talk does good.

January 13

In spite of improved attitudes in the last few days
Gordon Bell has climbed into school over the roof
after dark (in snow) with his infant brother; stolen
two shillings; left the classroom during craft and
gone to his father's house for something while I was
preoccupied; gone to the shops and stolen peas,
with Jones, during playtime; 'given' all his team
house points to get home early; and arranged
to stay away from school with David Gray. This
afternoon I heard of the plot and sent home for
him.

The story of 4C's moods, interests and crises according
to my diary is very much the history of Gordon Bell's
tempers. He is at the same time the most able, one of the
most likable and one of the hardest to handle boys in the
class. Most entries in the diary have a reference to him,
both because if anything interesting happens, or anything
is well made, he has had a hand in it, and also because he
is near the centre of any trouble or ill feeling. The record
of our hikes very largely concerns the way Gordon Bell

18

responded. I have usually tried to include him as often as possible since his need is so great, and any progress I make with him immensely benefits the whole class.

November 14

Today we went on the moors. It was rather a less successful trip than most of the after-school excursions. Perhaps nine boys were just too many. Perhaps it was too cold, although no one complained of that. We had intended to go walking, but very quickly it became obvious that they couldn't or wouldn't; they just wanted a base from which to play— exploring, chasing, etc. At the start everyone seemed discontented. Nobody would help collect wood for a fire or stones to peg the tent down. There were moans and grumbles about most things, even those they were enjoying. For example, we were all very eager and excited to grill sausages but, when the sausages were cooked, many found fault—'I like them done on the oven,' etc. It is necessary to ignore this, of course, although it is so galling since I am sure they are enjoying themselves and do not realise how unpleasant grumbling is. Gordon Bell has to run everything down and, as he is the leader, his attitudes catch on.

This, together with the steady bickering at one another they keep up—again especially Gordon Bell— the sneers at others' enjoyment and the unwillingness to co-operate in jobs like carrying firewood and building shelters, must be symptomatic of the deeper unhappiness they feel that present pleasure does not do away with.

I do not mean to give the impression that all was unhappiness; on the contrary, they all liked it and all begged to go back. But running through the fun and excitement (several had not been in the country before, none had been on the moors) there is a vein of discontent and malice, a need to gang up on others who are enjoying something and to jeer at a child who has found or made something.

We spent the day climbing bracken fells, exploring a beck, playing hide-and-seek and walking to a moorland village. They seemed to enjoy the bleak emptiness of the moors—its wildness giving scope for their wild turn of behaviour. Unlike many children they would probably prefer it to parkland. From time to time we broke up to go exploring. There was little real danger and most were unwilling to go far from me. Gordon Bell and Robert Box disappeared and later I discovered they had made a fire—dangerous, but they had not meant harm.

Most of the boys were rather nervous of the country at first, one extremely so. Gerald Brown was afraid of trees, sheep, a marsh, anything and nothing. He often wanted to hold my hand and talked constantly of disaster. At school he is not especially nervous or insecure, although I realise now that he is often more aware of the consequences of an action than the others. He does warn them quite often and is, in this way, the most mature. Today's haunted feelings are the reverse side of this coin. In spite of this his enjoyment of today was, I would guess, most like my own, in looking, sensing and just being there.

Gordon Bell, it is increasingly obvious, is the chief trouble-causer. He seems always to have a new friend; he is often amusing and generous to friends and very much the leader. Today he seemed to pick on each child in turn; most of the unpleasant bickering started with him. Each of his antagonists backed down in turn after a little opposition, until he came to Keith Jones, who is a match for him. Jones retaliated and there was a proper fight. Immediately we had two gangs and the day seemed to be in ruins.

Bell gets away with this so often because there is always someone willing to be on his side—if he smiles they come running.

Today it was Smith, Taylor and Bell versus the rest for the remainder of the day. Later I pointed this out to Bell. I think he understood and was abashed, but perked up and was soon friendly towards even me. When he believes I am wrong he is defiant and wholly unmanageable. He seems to need someone to fight with just as strongly as he needs a friend. In the classroom or out of it he is usually involved in a fight and can often make out a case for being wronged ('. . . This other kid was hitting my friend . . .'). Because he is quite intelligent he can discuss his quarrels and to do so has a beneficial effect if he feels I have a case.

Gordon Bell's background is very poor; to survive at all is his achievement. His parents are now divorced. For some time, however, he lived with them while the father's present (second) wife shared the house. Gordon is the eldest of four children, some of them coloured and some belonging to these two wives. Finally the first wife attacked the other woman violently and left the house. The father, according to Gordon's mother, turned against Gordon, blaming him for every trouble, even the break-up of the marriage, and she at last took him away to live with her. Most of the Bell children, scattered as they are through the school, are problem children, pilfering and behaving violently. Their father, an unemployed though apparently prosperous man, encourages them to lie and deceive the school about free dinners, etc. Unfortunately for Gordon, the house adjoins the school and he is often sent for by his father, although he always refuses to go.

Before I knew his history I used to wonder why he walked by this house stiffly, eyeing it sideways but boasting (as he still does) of his father's car, cine-camera, etc. He now lives with his mother some miles away. When she came to school once after I had realised the situation, I suggested that Gordon should go to the school nearest her new home. She begged that he be allowed to stay where he was. He would soon leave for the secondary school anyway and she might have to give up her home. She seemed a pleasant sympathetic woman and Gordon is very attached to her. He says, though, that she is 'never in of a night' and he gets his own meals. He often brings to school coins and flags that he gets from the foreign sailors who call for his mother.

Knowing this background makes it possible to tolerate the endless trouble and unhappiness he causes. His passion is football and he is quite talented. We fit in three games of football a week since the boys demand and need it. But every game except one has ended in a furious fight, centred on Gordon Bell. He keeps his temper for the first fifteen minutes; then, as his excitement rises, win or lose, he picks on the boys who tackle him and after the game hits them. I have tried both putting him in goal and sending him off the field, with a little short-lived success. The only thing I have not tried is to stop his football since this would be to take away the thing he comes to school for.

Last week a more dangerous incident arose through his football. All the boys turned against him when he was unfair in picking a team. This was most unusual since he commands allegiance where he wishes, and I was hopeful he would learn from it. Instead, when another boy provoked him, he attacked with a knife. Luckily it was flat-ended and his stab did no harm. For the next hour and a half I stayed with him and he began to talk more freely about himself. During dinner he shyly told me that he had been 'sent to hospital because of his temper'. It appears that two years ago, in a fury, he pushed a child under a car. The child was unhurt, but the driver had stopped and shouted at Gordon, who then threw a stone through the car window. Following this he was sent to a convalescent home for some weeks.

Although he is often so hard to live with there is much to like about Gordon. I believe I am lucky that he has rarely chosen me to quarrel with. While I am constantly protecting others from him, blaming him and seeming to be against him, he sometimes makes deliberate and thought-out overtures to be friendly with me—he asks me to go to the baths, to talk about my family, etc. Only once did I mishandle him to the point where we both became thoroughly upset and nasty, as the following note from my diary will show.

November 21

A small group—Bell, Robinson, Jones and Jackson—went to the reservoir. The succes or failure of the outing was always in the balance due to Gordon Bell's ill temper. However, I persisted in trying to avoid a flare-up. For the last hour he took his gang off into the woods and I saw little of them. On the way back in the car Gordon turned very nasty and, since I foolishly played a little joke on him, I bore the full force of his mood. He began to taunt the other children (having made sure first, with whispers, of Bob Robinson as an ally), to hit and threaten them. We were all tired and I warned him to leave them alone. He became more violent and began to sing dirty songs, and to whisper similar jokes to Robinson and to scream with laughter. I tried to talk him out of it, then to threaten him. 'Well, put us out of the car, we don't care. We'll come by ourselves next time, won't we, Bob? Look, here's a bus stop, put me out.' He began to shout of how he would break up any car that didn't give him a lift, and to talk and behave more and more wildly. The rest of the journey was hell, with Bell contradicting and mimicking me, quite out of control. We parted with very bad feeling.

More than most children he would benefit from a settled, stable class; the irritability and eagerness to quarrel of most of the other boys here is an extra serious handicap to Bell. He does not really belong in a C stream; his arithmetical and written-English ability would get him into the B class if he were properly tested. When he came to this school, two years ago, his teacher at that time says that for the first two weeks he was quite mild, he worked well and was plainly superior in ability to the rest of the C class in which he had been placed. Then he seemed to go to pieces and has been a problem ever since. I wonder if it took him a fortnight to realise what sort of children he had been classed with and if he has reacted violently ever since.

September 16

When we tried a play today there was no co-operation at all. Simply squabbles and fighting; and yet they were so eager to begin.

September 24

I suggested yesterday that they bring old cloth, curtaining, etc., for play costumes. Full of enthusiasm, several brought bundles today, jewellery too for making knights' costumes, crowns, etc. They like the idea of a jewel box.

October 1

The jewel box is empty; every single thing has been stolen—my fruit-gum-jewelled crown too.

When children are poor in the usual learning skills of reading, listening, observing and making, drama has an especially important place in their classroom. It is a natural extension of one of the things that many of them do well—playing. Even less than most can anti-social children be talked into learning. Listening is too static, reading too difficult, they are too little organised to learn much by watching and the opportunities are too rare for seeing worthwhile things. 'Living through' experiences in drama can be just right. As a situation for learning the things they lack most—self-control, understanding and awareness of others, and group discipline—it is unrivalled and it offers these things in an active though controlled way.

The process in which the child learns to so discipline himself as to co-operate in a creation with other individuals is surely one of the most valuable situations we can put him in. In addition he can be given facts and information as and when they are needed. If maturity is the aim, drama must be an important aid. The child's emotions, imagination and intellect are all enriched as he learns about himself and his colleagues—about people, in fact. But play-making is as difficult as it is valuable; movement, vigorous action and excitement are added to the usual classroom problems with unco-operative children who cannot organise themselves to do the things they want to do. The effort and energy required to bring thirty difficult children to do something worthwhile in these circumstances is enormous.

For most of the children in my class their previous experience of drama had been sufficient to make them un-self-conscious and eager. In the infant school they had been under the influence of a teacher who did a good deal. Some had been in her Christmas play and remembered it in detail. In the junior school there had been no plays or acting until last year, when, according to their teacher, 'they made their own and got on with it.' There had been neither assistance nor interference from the teacher, and they were eager to do it again when I discussed it with them. We tried it; the plays were not really attempts at telling stories, or being other people, or dressing up. There was certainly a great release of energy, though they did not create anything. Plays seemed rather excuses for free-for-alls, watched by the rest of the class. Invariably, whatever the subject matter, half-a-dozen boys would tumble through the door saying a few unintelligible words and then the wrestling would begin. Some minutes of fighting would pass until one of the wrestlers would jump up saying 'End of Scene I'. Exit all. 'Scene II—The monster comes back.' And the fight would begin again.

Thinking I might be able to use this to re-channel the energy with suggestions, I tried to discuss the plays with them. I explained the audience's obvious boredom and the unintelligibility of the scenes. The plays were a part of the general violence and aimless frenzy of their behaviour at the time. They were also too ingrained in the routine to be influenced. The girls' attempts—they never mixed—were no more interesting, though without violence. They merely continued the private play of infants, mother and child rôles, shopping or school. There was little attempt to be anyone else or to develop a story. Only the endless 'End of Scene I, Scene II' marked it out as a play for an audience.

Eventually I rejected these plays as being beyond my control and influence and started afresh with strong little tales. The first glimmer of success—moments within a play when most were contributing—was in a scene in which a queen died. The situation demanded quiet and a funeral. We got both in a long procession round the classroom with little acting and no dialogue, but discipline and response to ritual. The formality of the scene with its set phrases and hymn (God save the Queen!) was ideal for our abilities at that time and its success was no mere chance.

A serious mistake in these early days was to bring in costume—cloaks, crowns and helmets, and worst of all swords, since the children fought over these before the plays began and their attention was engrossed by them during the play. More ambitious and yet still successful was the attempt at *The Good Samaritan.*

November 16

The first two hours were very noisy and unsuccessful. The children seemed quite excitable (because it is Monday) and unwilling to settle down. Much of my morning was spent trying to calm them; they seemed surprised when I angrily told them they were ill-mannered—some seemed a little ashamed. I told the story of the Good Samaritan, intending to dramatise it this afternoon.

The afternoon began well, so we tackled the play in the first session. It was fairly successful, though almost completely lacking in discipline, and very noisy indeed. Compared with some things it was excellent. The idea of waiting to do their bit in the play when it is required seems to be dawning. Previously they have always played their part regardless of the story and other players. Today's improvement is enormous, although the play as a play is pretty dead. I started by asking 'Where shall we begin?' 'At the fight,' they chorused. It was a very successful approach; their enthusiasm was caught and kept. The first run-through was merely a fight; the second more ordered since we made it harder for the robbers to get at the Jew. The other two attempts were richer and, although they ended in chaos, they were gripping at moments.

It was an excellent theme for these children. The central violent point of the ambush was ideal to hang other quieter scenes on before and after. We had to begin this scene with silence and mystery, waiting for the robbery

27

to happen. Later the child playing the traveller complained of being hurt. By then we were sufficiently into the play for me to be able to say that if he got hurt again we would get other robbers.

In the opening scene there was always a little belief and absorption. It was immediately destroyed when the eight Roman soldiers teemed in to scatter the robbers and we were back to the free-for-all of earlier plays.

However, we had at last made the point that we could tell a long, even involved, story. The plays for the first time had a beginning, a middle and, occasionally, an ending whenever we got through to it. There was little real co-operation of course; usually each child was aware only of what he himself was doing and ignored the play and was rowdy whenever he was out of it. The story went better because several groups were isolated—Romans in one corner, robbers scattered about the room and girls at the inn in another corner. Only when all met did the play collapse. Apart from odd moments, when we could not help sticking to the story, it was quite like the old formless free infant play.

We finished with *The Good Samaritan* by showing it to another class. My own children were, of course, very eager to show it off and this led me to think that I would get more co-operation from them in the future. This expectation was not immediately fulfilled.

Few themes could suit us as well as *The Good Samaritan,* and when we next began with *The Pied Piper* it was a total failure. The full reasons for this are almost certainly too subtle and too many to discover with any exactness. With any children, but with these in particular, success or failure in drama, and periods like it, does not depend solely on the interest which the activity has in itself. Much depends on what has gone on before that day. They are never totally caught by the play itself. If the preceding arithmetic was ill-tempered, then it is pointless to try for self-control and purpose in a play. When boys have turned up having been caned or are in trouble with another teacher, then nothing will stop them wrecking our efforts. With drama, in this first term, I had always first to ask myself whether the moment was auspicious. If we seemed contented, then it might be worth a try.

Since so much depended on so many outside factors, success or failure in a play was practically outside control, and almost a matter of luck. The number of factors that could be structured to give success were at this stage few. With these provisos in mind we can say it is possible that *The Pied Piper* failed because it lacked real violence; there was too much need for dialogue that the children were not capable of—it is a talking play—and because I made the mistake of saying, believing drama to be the most popular current activity, 'If you don't want to be in the play, do this or that.' Only eight children began the new play with me; more came at odd moments of interest, but the rest made success impossible with their noise and troublesomeness. After this fiasco plays were not mentioned for two or three weeks.

When I felt sufficient confidence to begin again, the class choice of play was for 'a murder and a robbery'. We began *The Bank Robbery*. The play began well; once again we were to start with the killing and add to it. At this point we were visited by a drama tutor who, by invitation, took the play over. During the one and a half hours she spent with them their interest and enjoyment were remarkable. They willingly waited to contribute their part, offered suggestions for improving the play, elaborated her suggestions and in every way excelled themselves.

She left with the suggestion that *The Murder of Thomas à Becket* would make a suitable new theme since it needed violent, yet still players. This became our first real success in that the characters and situations were at times lived through by the children; that they worked at it over a period of time; and that it had an impact on an audience.

29

It also provided us with impetus to look up facts and pictures in books and to hear stories about twelfth-century England during the next three weeks.

Nothing happened suddenly. The first few attempts at the actual murder were chaotic, although the situation of most of the class kneeling in the cathedral, a few priests at the altar all neutralised by their parts, was ideal. The only free, moving children were the four knights who beat on the door and then strode up the aisle to the murder. Almost all opportunities for non-co-operation were eliminated—except giggling, and of this there was a good deal once the first impact was over.

It was obvious that if any real success was to come in drama the Becket play must provide it. To fail again would have meant that serious drama was out for a long time. We were on the verge of failure. Luckily a Christmas concert was announced. In the same week several of our ventures in other fields bore fruit; we seemed to be really making all-round progress. This gave me the opportunity to say to them that if we were to do anything in front of the rest of the school it would be this play—not a Beatle group or a romp, and that it would be done on my terms only; if necessary, I insisted, I would drop the play no matter how far it had gone.

This sort of crude bargaining—'Do it properly or else,' —cannot be entered into lightly with 4C. They are perfectly willing to drop anything, no matter how desirable it is, if it involves directed effort and seriousness. They simply have not been ready to be compelled into working, as opposed to playing, at a play before now. Partly this is through immaturity but mainly, I think, through past experiences. They seem sometimes to expect to have pleasant things taken from them—as though things they enjoy—football, painting, craft, physical education—have been used too often as bait for co-operation. Since it is never forthcoming they never expect pleasures actually to happen. Most children will put up with a bit of work or

discipline in order to achieve their end of fun; these children
seem to dare the teacher to take it away. Through repeated
failure they know that they are 'not the sort of children
who do this sort of thing.' Of course their enthusiasm
for these pleasures of school life is almost hysterical, but
they are not able to organise themselves sufficiently to
co-operate in bringing them about and so have been denied
them. No amount of coaxing or coercion brings certain
success. But because of the several different successes we
had recently had, and the increased confidence and self-
respect these brought, I said to them 'Do it well or not
at all.'

I have discussed this play in such detail because I
believe it to be the first time the class has worked together
to a common aim and the first time they have worked at
learning for the pleasure of it. The theme with the
situations it puts the children in was ideal for 4C. We
have several boys who cannot meet without clashing;
some were made knights, others monks, and the most
difficult boy of all was Becket. He had simply to walk in
procession, to lead the congregation in prayers and then
to be killed. Thus his anti-social opportunities were nil,
while his great ego was satisfied at being star of the play.

To make a real success of the play the children would
have to know a great deal more about the Middle Ages.
The play provided the motivation for this learning.
History for them is a kind of story and is acceptable to
them, as any story is, only in so far as the content is
exciting. The Becket play provided the background of
excitement, whilst I filled in the foreground of
unexciting historical detail to which they voluntarily
listened for several days. I know of no other way in which
I could have got the girls to listen whilst I lectured the
boys on their upbringing as pages and squires or monks.
Even more oddly, the boys became truly interested in the
plight of the lowest feudal order as I told the girls of their
dreary daily life as women of Canterbury. Divorced from

31

stories these details are utterly without the excitement demanded by 4C.

Some more able readers browsed willingly through real history books studying contemporary drawings of armour and plans of Canterbury Cathedral. These activities may be commonplace amongst children whose development has been normal, but such deliberate, continuous, voluntary learning was a unique experience for 4C.

The study bore fruit as the play progressed. It was astonishing to see Bob Robinson, who invariably scoffs and sneers at any form of make-believe or story-telling, slip into his character as Sir Robert de Polnay during a craft period and strut around the room unconscious of the rest of us. Later he told me of how he had been 'belted last night when I was practising my walk and they wanted to watch the TV.'

We added to the murder scene a long procession of white and red-robed priests led by a bejewelled-cross bearer. There were two silk banners next and, round Becket, a group of monks with lighted candles. With these props and a splendidly hollow recording of a cathedral choir in procession, the opening scene never failed to have impact. Particularly gratifying was the way in which it astonished an excited Christmas concert audience into silence.

Our progress in making effective props was another milestone. For earlier plays anything made was destroyed within hours. This time most objects survived and were even elaborated and used over two weeks without being much damaged. Several children so learned the lesson that care must be taken to avoid anachronisms in historical plays that they were heard to scoff at examples of wrong costume.

I can therefore claim that the play had many outstanding qualities that would be missed by any observer other than myself. If on the day it was publicly performed it lacked most of its feeling, and if the little dialogue it had ever had was mostly gone, it was still an extraordinary achievement for them. Even a casual watcher would have seen that the children had had an uncommon experience— had felt and lived through a time and an event outside their own lives.

To find out what they had learned about the process of play-making itself is another more difficult question that will need the next play to answer. It was enough that for two or three weeks we had followed a continuous integrated scheme of work when, for much of the time each day, we had been in medieval England. The ability of the medieval costume and trappings to feed the children was in contrast to the earlier attempts when they had merely confused and hampered the playing.

As children whose imaginations are truly impoverished they like history for perhaps the least worthwhile reasons —its violence especially, and surface colour. History cannot be said to have fed their imagination much. They read no real history, only comic strip versions of famous lives, and see inferior weekly stories on television. The occasional historical epics they see at the cinema may be the richest source of material they meet. Their home town itself lacks history of the type that would appeal to any child.

I was made aware of the result of this poverty of knowledge of the past when, quite without planning it, we stopped one day on a hike at a small town. The twelfth-century parish church was luckily near the sweet shop and we called in. Several children seemed and claimed not to have been in a church before. Their behaviour was most inappropriate and, had there been more than six, real damage would have been done. As they calmed down I pointed out that it was built in Becket's time and we looked at the stained glass, statuary and other features. It became apparent, as I talked, how ignorant of churches, their use and significance, they were. Much of my talk in the classroom had

33

presupposed a knowledge of things such as altars, tombs and stonework and must have been meaningless to them. Without such knowledge much of what I had asked of them in the Becket play was impossible—awe, reverence, horror at a murder in a sanctuary.

September 18

I have stopped 'teaching' arithmetic—they just get rowdier and are unable to settle down to written work if I do any discussion first. I shall concentrate on sums which they seem almost to enjoy although they are very resentful at first when I suggest work.

January 19

Robert Clark today announced loudly that he was going to do his maths instead of craft. He didn't, because he couldn't, and I was too busy to help— but what a change of attitude since last September . . .

The contrast between these two entries in my diary shows the improvement in attitudes as a whole and in this subject in particular. My first lessons in maths with 4C were occasions for clutching at the relative peace and quiet sums seemed to offer. Adding up and taking away columns of figures seemed to appeal to them once they settled to it. For the first week or so I would say to the class, which at this time was invariably rowdy and unco-operative, 'Turn to page ten and begin work.' If my voice had been heard they would subside for fifteen minutes into a reasonable quiet and concentration, a godsend in the restlessness of those days.

As I gained confidence and, I thought, knowledge of the handling of the class, I attempted to be a little more positive by beginning each period with a class discussion of some aspect of what we were to deal with. I kept this up for a while but with such little success that, as the diary entry records, I had to abandon it and go back simply to sums. Although we occasionally in those few minutes each day hit on something of value—I remember we invented a new number system and made a set of fraction cards—the all-too-frequent result was to unfit me and them for any further work or listening that morning.

Some weeks later I began introducing for a few more able children a set of cards with a more active, practical approach for work in groups or pairs. Although quite elementary and well within their abilities, and although some found them more interesting than sums, the cards required vastly more self-reliance and initiative than the children were then capable of showing. The card approach to such things as number, weight and distance was fairly sophisticated and much moving about the classroom was necessary.

If they highlighted the children's failings in being unable to work alone following instructions and using freedom to move meaningfully, how much more these cards showed my own failure to estimate their needs, abilities and limitations. In my searching around for a solution to the maths problem I had simply applied a formula that elsewhere had worked but which was here quite irrelevant. I recall being surprised and disappointed that it did not work. I have since failed many times in other subjects for the same reason of applying a ready-made solution without having thought the problem through. No doubt I shall do the same many more times.

The maths problem was, and is, just part of the greater problem of the education of difficult children. The essence of the task is to get them so to organise their abilities and knowledge that they are put into a position where they can begin to be able to cope with a situation in which learning is demanded of them. Every aspect of the school's work is subordinate to this aim of the social, emotional and intellectual growth of the children.

This is the reason why our earliest sums were to us as significant and useful as the most modern creative work in mathematics is to more able children. Although mathematically they are so inadequate and their use today seems to us indefensible, sums gave minutes of quietness and concentration and stillness, time to recuperate lost tempers, theirs and mine, and to prepare for whatever stresses would come next.

To be active in our work, to learn from doing things in a room where others were doing different things demanded far too much from these socially handicapped children. Doing mathematically meaningless sums was for this class at this point of time educationally more relevant than any attempt to go full-steam ahead in the direction of a programme designed to help children to discover meaning in mathematics.

Toward the end of the first term I was loaned ten copies of the Flavell and Wakelam books, *Primary Mathematics, Books 1 and 2.* This is a set text book that seems to be fulfilling our needs and is rewarding for several reasons. The work could be called modern in its approach in so far as it relegates computation to a lower position than in traditional school arithmetic, replacing it with more meaningful analysis of numbers and a practical concrete approach to such things as weight, volume and money. At the same time it does not abandon systematic bookwork.

In a sense it is a compromise between the two earlier approaches I had tried—the repetitiveness and manageability of the sums on the one hand, and the disastrous free-for-all of the cards on the other. The books ask much less of the children than did my cards in the way of social maturity and organised mental ability. From time to time each pair of children goes away from the group to do an experiment or to measure, to work with a plumb line, shapes board or other apparatus, but for much of the time they stay at their desks working on paper. At our present state of development this is an ideal compromise solution. As yet the number working away from the group has not been sufficient to disturb the rest.

Each week we seem to gain in responsibility and so more exciting things become possible. The set bookwork, without too much choice, has a steadying effect on the children who are as yet unable to cope with much freedom. The work is also in itself interesting enough to compel a fair amount of attention. Equally important for children smarting under the pain of too much failure is its simplicity—I can ensure that they get very little wrong and yet it is new and original enough to them to have status and intellectual respectability inside and outside the classroom.

Furthermore, a single text book common to the whole class is preferred by this group of children to any more flexible individually based programme. With a single text each knows exactly what the others are up to. They still like to see everyone else in the group take out a book and turn to a page they themselves have done or soon will be doing. A book has a certain hypnotic effect wholly beneficial in these circumstances. When they see other children pursuing an activity they would like to be doing, I often see them turn to those pages to find out when they will come to it, and the anticipation adds to the pleasure.

The approach of the book to maths is largely verbal and, although the children are asked to work in twos, written or even spoken instructions are too difficult to be followed without help, even by the most able children. Since we cannot attempt maths on a class or group basis, and even the pairs split up frequently as they fall out, each child demands individual assistance from me several times each lesson. This discussion between the two or three of us about the work is, I believe, the most valuable part of the course, perhaps of the day's work.

It is odd that this lesson, where contact between teacher and child has always seemed to me to be least (it was mainly between the arithmetic book or blackboard and the child), should provide the most rewarding situation for close discussion. In recent weeks they have settled down to asking for help when it becomes necessary, and to waiting for help to arrive. When I get round to them I read the book with them and then talk over whatever is to be done.

Some day, perhaps, they will accept help from neighbours, but at present even the closest friends rarely help each other much. I believe, in fact, that it delights a child to put his hand up to make me come across for a personal talk with him alone. In that it allows the child to feel a little powerful and a little more looked-after, this sort of individual tuition is very important to these children. The maths lesson unfortunately is almost the only time where it is yet possible to give it. Both the mental stimulus and the social contact of the talk with me make this one of the most rewarding periods of the day; certainly the children are at times eager for it to begin.

As yet they will not read even the most obvious short instruction. Perhaps this is partly laziness and in the coming weeks it may be necessary to wean them from it, but as yet I find the person-to-person contact, when it is thus asked for, so enjoyable and valuable that I am not eager to lose it. Children who in the course of the day hardly ever seem to talk or listen to me since I am so pre-occupied with general matters, and who are, in consequence, largely strangers to me, are intrigued when I crouch down before them with an abacus or number chart; they seem to open out at the intimacy of the contact. A great deal of the primary school child's desire to learn is, I feel, a desire to make contact with and to please the adults concerned. This probably is why Robert Clark, such a closed-up, determined-to-stay-apart boy, wanted to do his maths before his craft on January 19.

January 27

Jimmy McDougal asked last week if he could make
a 'bird book'. I was not at all sure what he meant,
but we made a little booklet with a wallpaper cover
and he went away satisfied. After a couple of days
I remembered it and asked to see it. He had drawn a
few shapeless birds from my encyclopedia; I made one
or two suggestions about naming and colouring the
birds. Next day almost by accident I showed it to the
class. It was a happy accident since the idea has
snowballed and each day this week has begun in a
frenzy of book making.

The frenzy of book-making lasted a fortnight and
produced three or four excellent booklets and a great deal
of hard work. Not realising it would catch on, but simply
to please him, I had displayed Jimmy's book that day
and casually said that if anyone else wanted to do one
I would help. I also set out a pile of old BBC pamphlets
collected over the years on nature study and history
and other subjects, saying that they might like to look
through them for pictures to cut out.

During the next few days book-making became our
chief activity. Practically everyone joined in with varying
success. I made piles of different sized booklets from
kitchen paper, staples and wallpaper. To have asked them
to make their own books at this stage would have
discouraged too many; it was largely the smartness of
the wallpaper cover, guillotined to shape, that attracted
them at first.

Subjects for the books were chosen mostly by
themselves, although several asked me what they should
choose. It is significant that only two or three boys—
those I would judge to be the most mature—chose
subjects they genuinely knew something about. Bob
Robinson chose prehistory; Gerald Brown chose the

39

Royal Navy ('I'm going to join it when I leave school')
and Gordon Bell chose history and famous people.

The rest mostly looked through the pile of available
pictures and found a series attractive enough to interest
them. I was more than satisfied at this since probably
for the first time ever some were consciously collecting
information and pictures round a theme and searching
through books of pictures.

The results of the work of many, perhaps most of
the children, was, by external standards, very poor—
pictures scrappily cut out, badly stuck in, not fitting
the page and badly labelled. But not all were like this,
and, since they could not do these things well, obviously
they needed the practice. The end-product is less
important than what happened to the child during the
making. Above all, every book was made from the desire
of the child to do it. They were made in the first session
of the day, normally craft time, and there was no
compulsion—except perhaps a little boredom and little
real alternative.

Unfortunately my own part in each booklet was slight,
since, as always during active periods, I was much too
busy keeping the thing going to be of much assistance to
individuals. No doubt, though, next time the fever of
book-making catches us, standards will have risen because
of the displays of the best and because of the experience
gained.

The most successful booklets I considered quite
excellent. These were those devised entirely by the child
himself—he drew or found pictures and wrote about
them what he knew. Next in merit were those made by
quite thoughtful children who came to me with a picture
they vaguely recognised, such as Nelson's flagship. I
would tell them its story or direct them to the appropriate
encyclopedia. They would go away and write their version.
Most children would simply stick in a picture and label
it 'A Sparrow' or 'A Horse', mis-spelt often, and several

could not manage even this. All, though, had had an exciting experience and a range of activities that differed in each case because each child's ability was different. There came first the claiming of an interest, then the selection and assembly of material with, occasionally, a search for facts to go with it. Every child was exercised by the arranging of his pictures on the page and some in the written work round the pictures.

Strangest of all, Sidney Robbins, a very apathetic lazy boy, came to me several days after the activity had worked itself out with a beautifully produced book of ships. Perhaps some of his apathy is fear of competing with the rest.

January 28

A visiting inspector remarked today on how pleasant the classroom is looking these days. It is true, and it made me consider how far we had come at this beginning of our second term. A good deal more now goes on in all directions—I feel less of a keeper and more a teacher. More too is made, and more lasts, and the resulting display makes for quite an interesting, cared-for looking room.

This improvement in the environment, created by the children, reflects the real improvement in their attitudes whilst in class—and, perhaps, outside. It seems worth reviewing in a general way what we have gained and perhaps what to aim for next.

The great change is in the relaxation in tension in the classroom and in the less negative attitude they show towards me. Almost all now seem to accept me as something of a friend, one who is on their side, and to admit my right to interfere in their school affairs without their becoming resentful and sullen. This is not to claim we are now well behaved. There is still a great deal of fighting and aggressiveness shown toward one another in the classroom.

Particularly bad is their crude jealousy of any very successful child. This week, for instance, Bob Robinson and Ken Salter have been bird-watching in a hide they made in the old yard. Although they know it is for all our use several boys whisper about destroying it at the weekend—it is fairly common to break into school by climbing the roof into the yard. More obvious still is the resentment against Peter Cole's drums and cymbals. Gordon Bell has already attempted to spoil them. No amount of success on their own part seems to reconcile them to the successes of others.

With fights in the room I am more able to cope. Having a better knowledge of those involved (usually the same half-dozen) I can separate the fighters, listen to an explanation and help talk out the trouble. They can see now that I am interested and am trying to be impartial; more important, they know that I realise there are frequently good reasons for fighting and these three-sided discussions are occasionally an interesting spectacle for the rest of the class. The other progress I have made in handling them is to be able to tell fighters to quarrel if they must but that we, the rest of the class, will keep out of it. 'It's Gordon's and Keith's fight—let us not take sides.' And sometimes this works. The most frustrating thing about their quarrels used to be the way in which an offence to one meant a feud for all. Now I see a 'wronged' child canvassing for support. This is progress, since they never needed to do this before, as automatically everyone else took sides.

The relaxation in tempers is beneficial outside as well as inside the classroom. I rarely see the children in trouble with other teachers and only two have been caned so far this term. There was a remarkable display of feeling last week when Joseph Banks was 'put up', as the children say, into 4B. He is a delicate boy, backward, with very little ability at school subjects. His mother is anxious about his being amongst my boys and believes he is doing no good with me. She was very pleasant about it, blaming the other children, but insisting he should be removed.

He was moved to 4B and there was a storm of resentment from the rest of 4C. I explained why he was going—several others wanted to go too, for the same reason. I talked for some time about streaming; they *know* they are graded as inferior but I had not realised how strongly almost all feel about being Cs. I tried to explain that 4B and 4C are no longer so different but that 4B and 4A especially have a larger share of good readers. This is pretty well true although it was not planned this way; from the school's point of view 4A, 4B and 4C are streamed by ability, 4C is definitely the lowest and all difficult and backward children have since been put in it. However, the results of the Christmas tests (standardised for fourth year) backed me up and they were reasonably satisfied. Since we are labelled 4C it is appalling that children like Gordon Bell, David Gray and Bob Robinson should be in this class. These three boys were very interested in the town's plan for reorganised secondary education since they may be treated more fairly. Thus the storm over Joseph Banks blew over.

The relaxation in temper is general, I think. Even Gordon Bell is less vicious than he was. A new development lately has been for him to sink into a sullen silence when offended. This is wholly to the good as far as we are concerned. Perhaps he has always been able to respond in this way. Perhaps, even, he has always behaved like this at home, but at school he has simply lashed out, whenever crossed, at everyone around him. Now it is sometimes possible to coax, flatter, and talk him out of his silence, even when he will not say what causes it.

Most gain has been made by Peter Cole. He is so much

less sly, less elaborately dishonest than he was. The times he had most to be watched were when he tried to gain his ends, often nasty, through niceness, and he would always go more than half way to meet trouble. Nowadays I sometimes feel he is being unjustly treated by the others, some of whom have not yet adapted to his improved personality. Some have noticed it of course—particularly Gerald Brown who said in an account he was writing recently of the class, 'Peter Cole was once the boss in this class as everyone was scared of him, but now he is softening up.'

February 22

Lately I have been able to leave three or four children in the room knowing I will not come back to damage and destruction. When I have felt a little group to be happy enough, I have deliberately this term left the room during playtimes with perhaps half a dozen children in it clearing up. Craft lessons first thing in the morning naturally leave it messy, but it used to be impossible to expect real help clearing up afterwards. Now I elaborately thank them, in front of the class later, when I come back to a remarkably cared-for looking room.

The state of the stockroom may sound a trivial matter but some days I have felt it is my greatest triumph. I have always allowed free access to it—it is a fair-sized room—and to its contents; consequently it is always in use, has been very much abused and has looked deplorable. Paper was stuffed in clay tins, brushes simply flung on to the top shelves rather than washed, tins and painting materials scattered everywhere. Clearing up made simply no impression on it, and the head's complaints were fully justified. During the holiday I came in and entirely reorganised it, labelling everything with colour and directions. For several days after our return I went in expecting a return to chaos, but still near half-term it is clean, well kept and, best of all, waste-free.

The attitude of the children to their own work is improving with their increase in skill. In craft they still sometimes work as frantically as ever as though the work would be snatched away from them any moment, but there is little wilful breakage and less hostility to the creations of others.

February 24

The fragile cubic shapes some of the boys made with drinking straws and pipe-cleaners—pyramids, cubes and polyhedrons (these are described as space-satellites by their makers) are still hanging up after two weeks. I was afraid they might not last the day, they so invite touching and are so delicate.

There is still little real continuity about their work and it is not done to any other purpose than the actual making. The solid shapes I describe above as surviving some weeks were made and put aside. I tried to talk to the makers a little about what they had done and how they had done it, but it does not catch on. There is no chance yet of much written work arising out of it.

Last week Gordon Bell and Fred Mullen made a farm model—they began it at least. We moved heaven and earth to make it possible, giving them all the big pieces of wood, balsa wood included, and shifting another model for space since they were so eager to make a good job of it. We had some interesting plans for it—a mouse maze, etc. The first day they did a remarkable job—trees, troughs, fields and fences and so on, but, not untypically, that evening they quarrelled and the project has fizzled out. The farm now stands derelict until Gordon Bell permits someone to finish it or move it.

This inconsistency is part of their immaturity, their inability to follow anything through in depth. I could of course insist that a thing be finished before another one is started. This works with most children and is I think quite fair, but, with us, any such insistence results in the deliberate destruction of what has been started. Once the first excitement has gone it is hard to pursue anything. The same is true of painting. We have so many half-finished craft projects in hand, it is hard to keep track of them. This is a very healthy state of affairs of course; craft lessons may be educationally fruitful even if there is very little fully ripe, polished fruit to be seen.

The children are often unable to cope with the richness of their opportunities. New ideas constantly come out and they immediately snap at the most attractive suggestion whether it is a bird bath or beat drums. It is a very wasteful system, but it does mean that when we do complete things they are quite exciting. For example, ideas came lately from the children for Daleks, a bird table, Tudor houses and a Roman Wall model. The first attempts at each of these (they are invariably imitated badly by others) were excellent by any standards.

March 3

Peter Cole is at last working to something like his real ability. He is a beat-group enthusiast and this week made an exceptionally good drum—plastic-covered and quite rich-toned. Next he devised a cymbal—a large tin lid, one foot across, suspended from a stand. This he pierced with lots of holes into which he inserted brass paper fasteners. The cymbal has a really fine sound. Now he is carving out and shaping some drum sticks. All this is incredible when I remember his state last term; he would neither make anything nor permit others to do so.

While we have an altogether much quieter, pleasanter time, the afternoons have still been noisy and bad tempered. The periods following the afternoon break have always required extra care if they are not to develop into a shouting match. Nerves seem to be frayed by three o'clock and tempers to get edgy, mine included; football has been a very frequent releaser of energies at this time or we have done simple things like drawing. The thing one might expect, listening to a story, has simply not been possible later in the school day since they are then at their noisiest and most uncontrolled.

February 16

Today I felt the time was ripe for a new step forward —or rather time for a test of what we have gained. Before afternoon break we painted very successfully and even cleared away without trouble. After break I quietly said that today, just for a few minutes as an experiment, they would listen to me telling a history story without anyone doing anything except listen. They have rarely listened to me before without plasticine, crayons, wood-carving and animals, and never in an afternoon. Today was different. For five or ten minutes nothing was heard in the room except my voice. They were not crushed into silence, just surprised that it could be so quiet. After the first few minutes the strain began to tell and in ten minutes children began to fall off chairs, open desks, and to take out toys. They enjoyed what I was saying but they had to be doing something else as well. But I felt I had made the point that quietness for listening is a good thing, and at 3.15 p.m. this was a remarkable achievement.

I have until recently seen very few of the children's
parents. One or two have been to the classroom door with
dinner money, but they never attempt to speak with me.
Parents are not welcome at the school itself and only
come up to complain. I have sometimes seen a few of my
children's parents at the gate with an infant brother
or sister, but they look so sullen, quite hostile
sometimes, that I have assumed that at best they are not
interested. All fourth-year parents were invited to school
in the evening of March 11 to hear about a scheme for
the reorganisation of secondary education and to meet
teachers. I expected little from it.

March 11

Nearly half turned up, in five instances both mother
and father. Although the really difficult parents did
not come, the fathers of several children with
problems of special interst were there—Mr. Robinson,
Mr. Brown and Mr. and Mrs. Cole even. I was very
surprised at their reasonableness and enthusiasm.
They were very diffident of course; they over-respect
schools and teachers but that is not their fault.
I finished the evening feeling most ashamed at what
I had brought myself to expect of them. If only we
had met sooner I would have been much more effective;
I should have been in a stronger position knowing
of their sympathy and their sometimes touching
interest in what was going on.

Perhaps the evening was an extraordinary experience only
because of the contrast with what I had let myself
expect. Relations with parents at the school are not at
all good, but this evening was very rewarding. Several
said that they knew 'something was up at school . . . he
won't keep away, he loves it, . . . what a difference.'
This was said of children of whom I would not have expected

it; Robert Clark, for instance, I never seem to speak to unless it is to tell him off. Bill Johnson 'never stops talking about it', but all I seem to do for him is to shrug him off and criticise him for being a nuisance. I have wondered why they persist in trying to be friends with me since, although troublesome, they are not in the same class as Robinson and Cole as mischief-makers.

Mr. Robinson would not go away; I talked to him first and he hung around the room for another forty-five minutes, going back to Bob's desk several times. I began by talking with him about why Bob was so aggressive, so cruel sometimes and so tense. I know that he has been in trouble with the police and is mixed up with real trouble-makers from the secondary school. Mr. Robinson told me he was surprised Bob was still considered difficult at school. 'It used to be true,' he said. 'We are a big family and the house is noisy and he can't read or play for the TV, but these last few months he's stopped going out after tea. He always wants to tell us about school, and he reads all the time.' I realised I had been talking about the old Bob Robinson and that in fact this term he had not been in much trouble. He still talks scornfully of teachers in general, but he is a very great deal happier with me.

A general comment of all parents, even the parents of Bert Walker, a brain-damaged child, was the 'niceness' of their child's bookwork. In fact the quality is not at all high. Only recently I attempted to get good-looking books; last term most written work was not done for the value of the writing but to provide respite from restlessness. Now the children are quite ready without a great deal of insistence to write tidily and to care for their books and to set things down neatly. But to hear 'Isn't this book nice!' over and over again was a surprise. 'Last year he only had one bit of paper with writing on—he was too untidy for books,' they said. Some fathers, Gerald Brown's in particular, had really been assured and convinced their child was an idiot, Mr. Brown, I knew, was surprised at Gerald's books and told me about last year. He was so obviously pleased, and looked it, that I felt quite happy for him.

In fact the big surprise of the evening for me was the way so many of the parents were so simply grateful that their child liked school and was making progress. The most difficult children's parents did not come, of course. I told the class next day, however, that any parent who had not been able to attend last night, could come any lunchtime or after school, and two have already done so.

February 8

Ken Salter and Bob Robinson made a bird table last week and asked me to put it in the playground. It was a very good one, copied from the current BBC pamphlet on Nature, and I agreed. When it was set up they wanted to watch it of course, so in the lunch hour we stood around and watched. No bird came within ten yards of it.

From these small beginnings our bird-watching has sprung. We talked at length about why the birds would not come, and in a few days we had begun to make hides. The final hide is in the park next to the school, on an island in the park—a bad place to have one, but the idea of having one there is so appealing and romantic I could not disagree. It finished up as a carpeted waterproof tent. For several days these two went in first thing in a morning 'to watch the birds bathing'. They kept records and studied books, allowed others to go in when they did not want to (with a very lordly condescending air) and finally gave up going in themselves. The enthusiasm may return when the weather warms up—just at present the classroom is the better place to be—but we shall see.

It was very worthwhile indeed. I realised early on that

its chief attraction for Bob Robinson was that it ensured
him my company and attention during lunch hours. He
longs to be talked and attended to; he is quite intelligent
and, if I get a chance to do so, it pays to attend to him.
The bird-watching was perhaps doomed when they realised
I would not always be around.

February 18

The bird-watching activities have developed further.
Several other boys, less able than the original pair,
want their own hide in the old yard. I am certain
that no bird will ever be persuaded to visit there
but they have made and set up a shaky table and built
a hide in one corner. I have mentioned the possible
outcome but they insist on sitting there each
lunchtime and are very content.

This had very little to do with bird-watching but it is
still a most enjoyable game. They slip into their hide
with comics—it is simply a den. I wonder if a club will
arise out of it?

We have kept animals this term with some success. We
started off with one guinea pig, were given another one
and then a child brought his hamster for us. These were
so obviously appreciated and so well looked after that
we bought two mice. All seemed to be going well until
February 26.

February 26

We have had the mice over a week. Yesterday a leg
of one of the mice was broken and today it died.
Today also the other mouse was found in its cage in
its death-throes, probably with a broken back. Jack

Owen had just put it in. He seemed excited and frightened and I would guess that he had done it deliberately, possibly experimentally. There is no point in pursuing it further, all the boys say that Jack Owen did it, would do it, is cruel, and so on.

I realised soon after getting the mice that they were too small and vulnerable for us. Most of the children were very good indeed with them but we do have several who, while they can be good most of the time, are in reality very deeply disturbed children. Jack Owen is one of the least able children there—judging by his performance, not perhaps his potential. He cannot read or do numbers or attempt to paint or draw. He makes things in craft and for the rest of the day goes dead unless I can allow him to go on making. He can be very sullen and rude to me if I mishandle him. Several times I have been told by his neighbours—he has no friends at all—that he kicks his dog and is very cruel to it. Probably one of these moods came over him while he was holding the mouse.

The children all love the animals of course—perhaps the mice especially since they were so lively. They had become part of the class routine—they were often in pockets during maths lessons and in desks most other times. Gordon Bell came to me one day to tell me that they had 'little human feet and paper ears.' He was keeping their diary too and felt their loss.

The other animals will probably survive because of their size. They are less exposed to impulse cruelty and, because they are big, can hardly be mishandled in secret should a child wish to do so. We keep records of their food and weight and diaries but most of what is said and written about them is, as yet, routine stuff. Gordon Bell's remarks were a hopeful first sign. Pets are rarely in their cages except in lessons when it is forbidden to play with them.

February 16

 The animals' food has provided a probable good
starting point today. Someone noticed that the food
we buy for them is mostly seed—corn, sunflower seed,
etc. When they asked me what it was, I suggested
we find out by planting a little. They were very eager
to do this and tomorrow we shall extend the
experiment a little.

The seed-planting was another snowball. I made out ten
science experiment cards to do with plant growth. We
have as the basic one 'What will come up when we plant
these seeds?', and the rest are hardly more difficult.
It was also an excellent opportunity of introducing the
garden plot I intend to start shortly; all the experiments
are relevant to what we shall do then and the knowledge
will be useful. We have already begun by digging over the
plot.
   The cards detailed experiments to find out such things
as 'Does it matter how deep we plant our seeds?', 'What
will happen if we crowd them close together?', 'Will the
plants grow if the seeds go in upside down?', 'What can
our germination plate tell us about roots and shoots?',
and several similar queries. There were ten groups with
three children in each group. We started that afternoon;
I risked their doing it all together and it went off
quite successfully. This is the first time they have
done experiments the result of which they will not see
for some time, so I was quite nervous of their reactions
and interest. The directions on the cards were apparently
almost foolproof. They have never followed written
instructions of any length before, but they so obviously
have benefited from the maths approach which is highly
verbal. I was needed to help very little and no experiment
was misunderstood.
   The 'Write all you have done to let the other children

know what your experiment is about' part of the operation was the least successful. They are still rather reluctant to write; perhaps by that time they were bored by it, or perhaps they just did not really understand what I was after and more help was called for. However, two or three groups tried and I shall try again with the rest when the first results begin to appear. Few children as yet look at or look after their experiment; I expect that this will improve when signs of life begin to appear and their interest is rekindled.

Although all of the children live in houses with gardens, few of the gardens are looked after and few children know the first thing about gardening. We are, in the huts, ideally situated to remedy this and some boys and girls are very eager to begin. We can now count on things outside the classroom being reasonably safe; none of my boys has recently broken trust and damaged anything out of school hours. As he threatened, some weeks ago Gordon Bell and his little brother climbed over the school roof after dark into the yard and took apples from the bird table, but did no real damage.

Now that co-operation, real co-operation as opposed to mere indifference, comes more readily, so much more becomes possible, especially in little points of organisation. For some time now since Christmas I have had none of the feeling that someone in the group was actively working against what I had in hand. No doubt much of my suspicion in the past was wrong; perhaps they were then not so much against me as just not assisting, and clumsiness and thoughtlessness can sometimes look like deliberate sabotage. Now, however, they often see the point of small organisational details and struggle with me to keep things going, as this entry shows:

February 10

I have discovered recently that the poetry books I
provided after Christmas, from the library, have
not been in circulation as I intended. They have been
kept in certain desks and, I am sure, rarely looked at.
Most children in the class did not know we had
them and I had forgotten several. I have organised a
Poetry and Encyclopaedia Corner (we already have a
Reference Book shelf but it does not work properly)
with a display of special books that are of temporary
though particular interest, such as *The Roman Wall*
for the model some boys are making. The books for
this corner are not allowed to go into desks. I have
made this rule about encyclopaedias before, but now
it seems to be working well and they are returned
after each reading.

The Poetry Corner is still working after two and a
half weeks and it is surprising how much more the books
are being read. The encyclopaedias now seem to be often
referred to on particular points. They were reasonably
well used before as reading books and it did not do to
over-insist on the not-in-desks rule since the result was,
as often as not, that some children read nothing at all.
Even more interesting is the new study of the poetry
books which are always in demand as private reading
matter. Sometimes there is a wail if none is available
or one is in a desk. Since they are before my eyes too,
I seem to read more poetry to the class. On occasions I
have been asked to read a poem. I do not put too much
value on these requests, although I agree to them, since
I have noticed they can be a cover-up for some less
worthy motive. Gordon Bell, in particular, knows that I
insist on silence when I read a poem and this means my
coloured felt-tip pens become available. It is no bad
bargain; poetry and silence in return for coloured pens.

The girls sometimes genuinely want to hear more. It is, however, hard to evaluate the situation exactly. It is clear that when I read poetry it means I have judged we all are in a receptive state; that is, they are relaxed and I am pleased. But which comes first—their calmness or my good temper? Sometimes I know the girls are flattering me into poetry reading.

September 14

At last I found a story to which the class listened fairly well. It was Wilde's *The Happy Prince.* Some seemed quite moved by it; perhaps its extravagant sentimentality appealed. It is quite a good story and I was very grateful for it.

All through September I struggled to find a story that would catch their interest but they were no more willing to hear what I chose than to listen to my arithmetic. In the first weeks I tried stories from the *Faber Book of Stories*—all good, tried and successful with anyone else. I simply had to read above the noise, knowing that few wanted to hear, though all were compelled to stay in the room. Most were willing to do this if they could have something else to do—paper cutting, crayons, plasticine, as well as sawing or drumming. The strain was enormous and at first, having failed to get the expected silence of normal children, I stopped reading. There was no improvement. They just did not want to hear and would not listen unless something else was offered with the story. And they do not move quietly; in whatever they do they are graceless and noisy. Since nothing I could do altered this, I eventually learned to accept all the activity and, as far as possible, to side-track the noisiest, like sawing, by issuing quieter equipment and, as a last resort, by allowing the two noisiest to work in the stockroom.

Thinking that perhaps I was reading stories they already knew I asked their previous teacher what he had read them. 'Stories from an old class-reader, or supplementary readers,' he replied.

September 25

For some days now I have tried the class out with Ian Serraillier's *Hero Stories*. The response is no better than with simpler stories. They appear not interested. Rosemary Sutcliff's *Beowulf* was a bit better in the gruesome parts, but the six ex-B class boys have heard it and will not give the others the chance. It is unbelievable the number of times they fall off their chairs; several chairs have been broken slightly, one completely, through their sitting on one or two legs. Last year they had iron desks.

Soon after half-term I began a high quality Western children's story, *Children on the Oregon Trail* by A. Rutgers van der Loeff. The story concerns a family of six children who set out with their parents in a wagon train into the American West. Soon the parents die and the children leave the caravan and set off alone into the wilderness. The story, a true one, relates the hardship and suffering they underwent before reaching Oregon several months later. The book was an immediate success in that several began to ask for it. There were the usual jeerers, particularly when anything happened that was emotional. Some seemed to have the superficial hardness that noisy teenagers affect in cinemas when such scenes are shown.

The story was ideal for this class in that its violence and the intensity of the suffering of contemporaries in a Western setting held them as nothing else ever had. This is not to say that the noise was appreciably less. By now the activities that took place while I read were habit,

57

a routine they would not do without. The story was also a difficult one, above the heads of several children who could not be expected to listen. But through the noise I knew most were listening, even the scoffers.

Bob Robinson's reaction to the story *Oregon Trail* is puzzling. He likes it, I know; he even settles down in his chair and does nothing but listen—and jeer. He seems to need to prepare for the next episode of suffering by standing outside it and forecasting what is going to happen, all in a loud voice and sometimes continuously, during the reading. When the violence in the story breaks through, he acts it and then lies back in his chair with a hard sneer on his face—truly unpleasant to see—and laughs 'Ho! ho! ho!' In the same detached way Robinson often talks about his old grandfather. He will tell me something quite pleasant about him, then finish with a very unpleasant, quite accomplished sneer about the 'doddering old man' or how 'he's going to die soon and become an angel.'

Later I began to wonder to what extent Bob Robinson may be deeply worried about death. His mother has a heart condition and talks about it in front of her large family of six. They have been broken up before when she went into hospital and this certainly worries him. When an uncle died he insisted on being told the details of what happens at a funeral—his interest was quite morbid.

I was quite unable to assess what the children had got from the story. They were unwilling to talk about it, to paint from it or write about it, and whatever effect it had inwardly did not show. It was a very long book by their standards and, by the time it was half through, it had become a looked-forward-to routine. 'Will you read us about those kids?' was a very welcome sound.

To exploit their obvious liking for animals, and to see

if they would accept a non-violent, comic adventure story, I next tried Hugh Lofting's *Dr. Dolittle* series. The story of the doctor who understands animal language and is kind to the point of being ridiculous had none of the qualities I knew to appeal to the class. I am not sure of the value of the book itself, but something of its good humour did get through to them. At the time I took it as a very happy portent that the class had relaxed sufficiently to enjoy a simple entertainment. Oddly, though, they did not realise that it was meant to be amusing. Even the most far-fetched incidents and creatures—the two-headed animal and the birds pulling the ship across the sea—were accepted without a smile by almost all. One boy, Ken Salter, who is well-informed, did ask seriously if such an animal as the Pushme-pullyou existed, but then burst into laughter. But they did enjoy it. One or two even borrowed it to read at home and some demanded more *Dr. Dolittle* books.

I had myself had enough, however, and the next book I tried was Mary Norton's *Bedknob and Broomstick.* This story appealed to me greatly and I had previously read it with considerable pleasure. The idea of a modern spinster as a witch who magics a bedknob to take three children through space and time is realistically and ingeniously told. By coincidence the favourite television series of the minute was about a modern American witch and, although this turned out to be a commonplace comedy series, the children saw enough link-up to be pleased and to anticipate some fun. Any such connection was valuable as a starting point. The bed takes the children through two disastrous, enjoyable adventures, comic yet frightening, as a preliminary to a trip to seventeenth-century London. Throughout the book there was considerable audience participation. The children in the story are easily believed in; they have a working mother and no father; they invariably cause trouble for adults and are irritated by their little brother, although they like him. He also happens to hold the key to the magic.

The story's ending is only half happy and it would be particularly hard for less able children to follow if it were not so well handled. The children's friend, the witch, decides to return to the seventeenth century with the magician whom the children had brought back from that time to her house. In the final scene the children in modern England go to the ruins of the magician's country house where they know the couple will be. It is a sad and confusing moment and I had expected it to go straight over the heads of 4C—no action, a difficult time concept, a farewell kiss.

December 18

The moments when I read the last pages of the book were extraordinarily moving. There was a dead hush till the very end. It was broken by a surprised shout of 'She's gone!' and 'It's finished', as they came out of their involvement. It was most rewarding. This was the only time that activity has stopped for a story. Several children remained standing at their desks with their heads turned and hands idle. It was almost uncanny.

To capitalise on the interest and insight into history gained from these last chapters of Mary Norton's book, I next chose a full-scale novel with a historical setting— Geoffrey Trease's *Cue for Treason*. It is a modern-style adventure story set in Elizabethan times with treason plots, disguises, man-hunts and plenty of threatened violence. At the time the book seemed wholly satisfactory; it was quite popular and the children seemed to identify easily with the two chief characters, a boy and girl of their own age. Their listening was usually polite and they seemed more involved than in previous stories. There was, however, no carry-over into other fields; nobody wanted to draw, paint or model anything from it and I cannot recall any talk about it. Their pleasure in hearing it was sufficient to make it worth while and it was not until I read the next book that I began to doubt the quality of their appreciation of *Cue for Treason.*

The new book was Henry Treece's *Horned Helmet.* It is a story of Icelandic Vikings and their pirating adventures. Beorn, the chief character, a twelve-year-old boy, is savagely treated by his community and particularly by his master Glam. He runs away but Glam catches him and we know he will be lucky to survive. A band of Vikings intervenes, humiliates Glam and takes Beorn away. In time he becomes a Viking raider himself but eventually outgrows pirating and settles down, a farmer, to protect his adopted father and mother.

The impact of a story of this nature, less an adventure than an account of the feelings and the growing-up process of an unfortunate child, was very marked on class 4C. From the beginning their involvement was deeper than with *Cue for Treason.* Beorn, in contrast to the other children whose trials are on a plane of high adventure, remote from Townend Estate, suffers injustice and misfortune without end and never really wins. The high points of the story, and there are enough to make it thrilling, come when Beorn is grudgingly accepted by the others, little by little, and when finally he comes to accept them and so to accept life.

It is a remarkable feat by any standards and to most of these children it was hypnotic. If they show any generalised feelings at all it is in believing themselves badly done by. Beorn was one of themselves, a person with their problems, and his resolution of them they found wholly satisfying.

Gordon Bell, in particular, was caught up in it, especially when the boy was being savaged by his master and ran away. Perhaps because I knew that, that very week, he himself had run away again from his father's house to his mother's, out of town, I watched his reaction. This chapter meant a very great deal to him; always when a character in a story is harmed by another he calls out and repeats intensely, 'If they did that to me I'd kill them . . .' This time, when Beorn is rescued by the Vikings and offered revenge on Glam, although he did not take it, Gordon glowed with intense pleasure. Even if the other children did not see themselves so plainly reflected in Beorn, the story of a child victim triumphing over bullies and other misfortunes held a great deal for them who seriously believe themselves unjustly treated by home, school and the world at large. Out of the story came, quite spontaneously, paintings, attempted models of ships, two large models of the spot where Beorn, Glam and the Vikings met, a play, shields and an interest in the Viking gods and heroes.

February 24

I found the hamster dying in its cage at four o'clock yesterday and removed it without anyone knowing. Peter Cole had been playing with the hamster on his desk shortly before four o'clock. He seemed then to be playing with it quite normally, even affectionately—I heard him talking to it. It was he who killed the other hamster last term, I am sure, although we had no proof and nothing was said openly.

It was obvious on the following day that Peter Cole's behaviour was strange. He did not approach or speak to me once before break. I saw him listening to the children's talk of the hamster not being in its cage and he seemed very 'conscious'. Although nothing was mentioned directly, I admit to being distant with him, and during the day there was a very definite return of his old anti-social and aggressive behaviour—for instance he poured paint into the fish tank. Perhaps this was a simple retaliation to my cool attitude.

At the start of the afternoon break he went into the stockroom to sweep up. Glad to have him there, I did not interrupt after break and we heard him moving things about inside.

He did not reappear until the other children had all gone home at 4.5.p.m. I hurried them off on purpose to get a chance to talk to him. I thanked him for the extraordinary job he had done in there; for the first time since September it had been really thoroughly swept and everything replaced. Patently this was some sort of gesture; possibly the hanging back was in order to be thanked, but by the time we had finished talking, at 4.30 p.m., he was obviously as relieved as I was to have had it out.

I began by saying to him, almost casually, that, as he knew, the hamster had not escaped but had been killed. He interrupted to say everyone knew it had escaped, they had all told him so. I had allowed them to think so, I replied, since if they knew the truth they would be very hurt and angry with him. We mentioned the other dead animals. After a good deal of roundabout talk by me, keeping all reproach out of my voice and words, he admitted it.

At first it was just '. . . *I* didn't hurt the *mouse* . . . or the hamster,' but then he began to talk about it more freely. I told him of my real surprise that he had done it now, since he was so much happier and better liked. He told me he had come to enjoy school and that he himself had noticed he was in so much less trouble and fewer fights than before. It is true that the other children now largely accept him. Eventually he said quite spontaneously, 'I could get a rabbit, or a chicken, from my uncle who breeds them.'

By now I could sense his relief at talking this out; he had lost his unchildlike air of defiance and was almost pathetically vulnerable. At last he said, 'I'm always doing it, breaking things. Sometimes I just break my records, I don't know why.' After some more talk like this, as little conclusive as such talk ever is, he went away quite lightened and seeming more truly happy than I often see him.

This talk, inadequate as it doubtless was, was a considerable relief to both our feelings. I had been particularly angry with him, partly because of the affection for the hamster all the children, including Peter himself, had felt and for the shock they had received when it too, along with so many other good things, was lost. But especially I was surprised at this reversal in the behaviour I had recently come to expect from Peter Cole.

From the very start Peter Cole has been the most frequent source of ill-feeling in the class. Gordon Bell, his closest rival in trouble-making, can be very difficult but his misbehaviour is more predictable, easier to understand and, no matter how gross, it remains childlike; Bell also stays popular with most of the rest of the class no matter how much he bullies and gets them into trouble, and his behaviour therefore seems healthy. None of this was true of Peter Cole. He was the most violently disliked boy in the school. The children would have nothing to do with him except under threat; frequently he would say, 'Be friends or else . . . ', and only John Wilkins would submit even then.

Gerald Brown, a sensitive, quite intelligent boy, said to me last term after one of the then daily incidents centring on Cole's viciousness, 'I remember the day Peter Cole first came to this school. We were in the infants and he was standing by the railings over there. I said to myself that we were going to have a lot of trouble with that boy, and we always have. I've always been in his class. It's awful.' Gerald Brown has had every reason to remember his prediction of five years ago.

My early diary has an almost daily comment on

Peter Cole.

November 6

Straw in the clay bucket; Peter Cole again.

November 9

. . . Later I discovered that the hands of my desk
clock had been twisted off. The glass was broken
last week. Peter Cole was last seen with it, but he
wasn't around. Had he done it and disappeared?
He had.

All the members of staff had funds of stories of his
callous brutality to children in their classes. The infant
staff too had memories of his bad influence. Only one
teacher there had a happy memory of his being thoroughly
engrossed in a Christmas play. Much of his behaviour
was still infantile—he would be on his back in the field,
kicking and howling, for perhaps twenty minutes, when
left out of the football he refused to join in. At other
times his attitude and behaviour would be like that of a
teenager in revolt.

November 19

Miss Thompson, the student, tells me that at last
night's practice match after school Peter Cole was
whistling and shouting insolent and crude remarks
at her from the sideline. The staff, hearing about it,
were furious. I talked to him at length about it. He
seemed touched—he always does if spoken to, and
I suggested that people who are sorry sometimes
apologise. He did so, to Miss Thompson's satisfaction.
Later the head heard about it and Peter was caned.
    Miss Scott (the new young teacher) now says that

when she came to visit the school last term he winked, whistled and was rude to her in the corridor. She did nothing, assuming it to be normal practice.

He seems to have picked up much of this attitude to women from his brother. This eighteen-year-old has a beat group and Peter says he plays with them on Saturdays at teenage clubs. His size—he is overweight—and his inappropriate dress would make him stand out anywhere but there. He sometimes comes to school in this brother's clothes—high stiff collars, high heels, string tie, etc. Many children's mothers have been to the school to complain of his treatment of their children here and in the streets at home where he is equally feared. He seems to have only two attitudes, both repulsive—a defiant insolence with curled or pouting lips or an ingratiating smirk. Two very old members of staff assert that in all its history the school has never had such an unpleasant, more dislikable child than Peter Cole.

Over the years several letters have been sent to his home, by post since he is untrustworthy, asking his parents to come up to discuss him with the head. None had any response. Then last term, soon after he killed the hamster, he seriously attacked some small girls in the playground, and a letter was sent to his family saying that he was being referred to the educational psychologist with or without their consent. This too was ignored and so it was thought that a 'phone call to his father's place of work (he is a garage foreman) might get response.

Within an hour the father arrived at the school, indignant at not having heard till now of this history. He claimed that his wife must have kept the letters from him. The truth is that Peter's parents have long ago lost control over him and now make feeble excuses for him: 'Everyone has a down on him here because of his London accent.'

No real help was forthcoming. The psychologist

examined him with tests for a whole day and pronounced that he was a naughty boy but that nothing could be done until he did some real harm.

It was always obvious to me that the boy was working far below his real ability. He talked well, mainly of beat music, and had a good vocabulary, but he could only just read and his arithmetical ability was even lower. Any paper work he did looked deplorable but there were occasional signs of reasoning and fair intelligence. He sometimes had odd flashes of inspiration in making or doing things that he had pursued for some time. The first of these was painting pebbles we had collected at the seaside. This might have been a low-level activity but it meant a great deal to him and he did it for a whole day.

October 13

Peter Cole stayed in the painting corner the whole morning painting large pebbles we had brought back from the seaside. On some he made quite fine patterns; I had nothing to do with it; when I saw he was absorbed I left him alone. When the other children complained that he was not working I got him to slip into the stockroom and continue there, out of sight. He continued until four o'clock. This is the first really trouble-free day he has had.

At other times he has begun and wished to continue making some special thing—in wood, cardboard or paint—well above the general level of creativity of the class. The inspiration for these things always comes from himself; I do not remember ever successfully planting an idea, though I have helped him execute many. Of course since the children dislike him so much they are very aware of anything that looks like special treatment. There have been several 'rebellions' because of this but it has usually been possible to placate the ringleaders (Bell or Gray) and allow Peter to get on with the one thing that he has put anything into in perhaps a week of school.

That such a primary school history should have a happy ending is so improbable that it seemed too much to hope for. I thought all last term I had made no real progress with him; I simply tried to protect the others from him. Since the end of Jamuary, however, something of a revolution in his behaviour has been felt in the classroom and in the school. Whether his new attitude to daily craft (as opposed to irregular spasms of activity), to his mathematics, to bookwork in general, to other children, to sport even, came first or came suddenly I cannot say. I realised some weeks ago that he was so much more content and constructive and in all these things he gains apace. He must have been improving since before Christmas but only recently has it seemed spectacular.

On the evening parents came to school, Mr. and Mrs. Cole were there, and apart from one or two last-ditch excuses, they were wholly agreeable. They assured me that at home Peter is so much happier ('But he always was.') and that he talks such a lot about school. He is quite altered, it seems. The head made a special point of talking to them about Peter's new self, as he considers it, and all seemed set for a happier future.

That there should be no setbacks would be inconceivable. In fact Peter is still often in trouble but since it is so much milder it seems quite pleasant trouble. His killing the hamster shows how deeply his disturbance goes. It would be strange if he were to come through the experiences of the past few years without serious damage to his growth as a person. But he does get on so much better now with the other children; he was certainly very eager the other evening that they should not know what he had done—a positive sign of his desire to be accepted by them.

April 10

The headmaster came to me this morning to tell me
'The funniest thing in years.' Tom Williams was at the
football match last night on the field. He sidled up to
the head after a while and said with a sideways
smile, 'I'll bet you'll be glad when it's July and I
leave, won't you?' The head laughed in agreement.
Tom went on,'Hey! What would you say if I stayed
on another year, eh?' and he doubled up with
laughter.

I was just as astonished as the head was amused with this
story. That Tom Williams should ever be sufficiently
detached as to see himself and his relationship with
anyone, particularly the head, from the outside, is cause
for astonishment. Some teachers find him the hardest to
handle, though not the most malicious child in this class,
and he has a continual running fight with the head.
The truth is that he is almost never vicious but that he
lacks almost any self-control. Just as he often cannot
control his limbs, he cannot help his bad effect on people,
and he can never understand why they do not like him
when he means no harm. To describe him is very difficult.
In appearance he is skinny and sometimes ragged (although
this has improved) and a lost, waif-like air typifies him.
His home life seems very poor; he talks repeatedly with
great affection of 'our baby'—the latest of several. As a
baby he is said to have had some disease which has
affected his motor control and nervous system. He is
very highly strung, nervy and never still. He tells me often
of his nightmares, his bed-time fears. Once he came
rushing terrified into the room, 'chased by three fingers',
which he continued to see for another hour.
If as a child I find him pitiable and very likable, in a
classroom he is the ruin of order and quietness. He finds it
quite impossible to sit still or to listen; he has heard none

of the stories I have told and read. The trouble he causes is apparently always unintended. As I read he thrashes about in his desk, standing up, knocking his chair over, wandering about to get anything in the room that catches his eye, or to take it by force from another child. He is totally unaware of the disturbance he is causing. I stop and tell him to settle down; it has no effect and I repeat it angrily. 'Tom, you have banged your desk lid again four times and disturbed everyone around you.' He shouts back, harshly, 'What's the matter with you? I am sitting down, look, and I never touched my desk, or them!' and he will wave his fists or hit his nearest neighbour. To argue at this stage is useless; the other children just accept him and say, 'He's a bit mad.' He seems, in fact, quite incapable of seeing either himself from outside or another's viewpoint in anything, When he 'takes things'—steals them—he seems not to know that they belong to anyone else and that those whom he has robbed will feel hurt. He takes openly, from my drawers as well as other desks, pens, toys, books and plasticene. This year, since he has come to like me, I have been able to talk him into returning things with no ill-feeling, but if he has had a thing a day or two he forgets it ever was not his and real trouble flares up.

This I have always claimed for him is part of his gross immaturity. His attitudes and actions are in so many ways infantile. He reads silently well enough, for instance. But to read aloud he deliberately adopts the worst reading-aloud tones and defects of small infants, and he cannot understand why the others laugh at him for it. If we have a play he must be the announcer. He stands stiffly at the front, hands by his side, and in an artificial calling-out voice, splitting each word into monosyllables, makes nonsense of the announcement. He did this, he says, in the infants, and his style now is exactly what was then pressed on him.

Certainly Tom Williams is the prize example in this class of a child who has gone through the junior school with a closed mind, taking nothing from it and growing not at all since the infant school. He is, of course, greatly disliked by the staff; one teacher who takes the class once a week will not allow him through her door. The babyhood ailment may have caused many of his troubles but little contact has been made since to help.

Early on in the year I began to realise that he also was the victim of his failings as well as myself. I found him unusually responsive to kind words and, while clashes continued as much as ever, especially with others, I began to have some control over situations in which I was involved. By a lucky chance one day a painting he did caught my eye (he usually refused to paint) and quite carelessly I said I liked it. He has repeated that painting exactly very many times since—twice in one period some days. Largely out of that remark his belief in himself as a painter has grown and he now has something of a reputation for it. On different occasions he has written in diaries and said, 'Our teacher says I am a good painter. I like painting.' He always asks me if I still like his painting.

His other great success has been in mathematics. His written work can look appalling but again, luckily, I early on praised his book. Now I am compelled every day to do the same—it is usually worth it—and to give him extra attention with it. He enjoys it so much that his skill which was negligible now equals that of most in the class.

He is, I believe, gaining just as rapidly in social skills, as when, for instance, he spoke to the head, and with a little sympathy next year should achieve normal relationships in his new school.

To generalise about and to abstract principles from the experience of the past two terms will add little of value to the preceding pages. My characteristic modes of thought will have revealed themselves clearly enough through my account of the difficulties and pleasures that have arisen with 4C.

I would, however, like to add a brief reference to the contribution made by reading to the eventual clarification of some of the issues. Obviously, as I began the year unaware of how unusual a year it was to be in my teaching life, I approached the problem from the very first with as open a mind as possible and worked intuitively without reference to what others have written or said. Since, however, I first began to find my bearings and gradually to become more objective about my problems, I have become increasingly respectful of the work of A. S. Neill. Returning to his books I have rediscovered as proven fact those things that had appealed in previous readings only instinctively.

And so I have tried always to believe that when a child has misbehaved, however grossly, sometimes even frighteningly, he has had a reason, perhaps undiscoverable, and that he also would rather his life were trouble-free and happy. If there is deep hostility that cannot be controlled or express itself in an acceptable form, I have found it quite useless to be shocked at crudeness or violence and even more stupid to retaliate with more violence.

All this sounds too idealistic to be true. Of course it is. Failure to live up to one's ideals is only human; I alone know how often I have fallen short. But the children themselves have learned to accept, even to forgive, such failure. When, as always happens toward the end of the second term, we began to be irritable and easily aroused, there was consolation for me in seeing the ease with which the children had come to return good feelings for bad. If they are ever to learn to cope with their own bad feelings it is not unimportant for them to learn to put up with the failings of others.

Inevitably, being the kind of teacher I am, most 'acceptable forms of self-expression' come in the period

72

we labelled craft. It has included those things which normally come under that heading—puppets, clay, paint, modelling—but also any form of activity from gardening to tidying up the drive, which the child claims to be creative or merely useful. With another teacher or with other children, some other formula would have been found. Whether indeed my approach, in so far as it is distinctive, can be held to apply to other situations, I cannot really tell, since a change of circumstances would alter the interpretation of 'facts' and one's approach would alter accordingly.

I have frequently and unwillingly found myself in arguments with other teachers on this matter of the approach to be taken toward other children. Can one assume, for example, that 4B next door makes trouble as unwillingly as I believe 4C usually does? Would these normal children rather be punished than be endlessly forgiven and understood? Possibly, even probably, they would.

My experience with 4C assures me only that they, disturbed and emotionally deprived as many are, cannot cope with punishment, especially physical punishment. They do not have the resources to put up with it. Many times I have been astonished at their deep bitterness, and at the violence which is created, if they have been roughly treated by a member of the staff, no matter how they have provoked it. It has taken over an hour for a caned child to be able to sit down and to stop muttering violent threats on returning to my room. This reaction cannot be expected of normal, well-adjusted children who seem able to take caning in their stride, whatever harm it may do to them at a deeper level. But even for 4C, too much sympathy and understanding is hard to put up with. I am sure that of late they appreciate it if they find they can 'needle' me into anger and, having done so, let it go. This seems a reasonably normal state of affairs.

For the future my broad aim is to consolidate what I have gained and to let the gains—intelligent use of freedom, skills, interests and other kinds of learning—grow as naturally as possible out of whatever we do. Inevitably for me the most enjoyable and therefore the most fruitful part of the day will come with literature. A more integrated approach may be possible, unified through a book; we have already had hints of it this last term. The social skills learned in the classroom will, I hope, be tested and proven outside school on hikes and, where possible, hostelling at weekends.

This book was originally published by the Research Committee of the Institute and Faculty of Education, University of Newcastle upon Tyne as one of a series of reports on work done in schools and described in fine detail for the interest of teachers.

The following titles in the series are available from the Institute of Education, The University of Newcastle upon Tyne, St. Thomas' Street, Newcastle upon Tyne NE1 7RU.

1. **The Privilege of Language** Free verbal expression work in self-chosen groups by underprivileged girls in an urban secondary school.

2. **No Master's Voice** Free expression work in prose and verse by boys failing academically in a selective school.

4. **My Book My Friend** Individualised and organic reading materials and methods with 12 to 13-year-old ESN girls in a day special school.